SOCCER

By Cindy Trumbore

Modern Curriculum Press

Credits

Photos: All photos © Pearson Learning Group unless otherwise noted.
Page 1: Jed Jacobsohn/Allsport Photography. 5: Larry Voigt/Photo Researchers, Inc. 6:
Stephen Dunn/Allsport Photography. 7: Gary M. Prior/Allsport Photography. 8: Steven
E. Sutton/Duomo Photography. 11,12: William R. Sallaz/Duomo Photography. 13:
Kyodo News. 15: Corbis-Bettman. 17: Damian Stohmeyer/Sports Illustrated Picture
SLS. 18: Damian Strohmeyer/Michael O'Neill McGraph Arts & Graphics. 19: Doug
Pensinger/Allsport Photography. 20: Shaun Botterill/Allsport Photography. 21: Clive
Brunksill/Allsport Photography. 22: Chris Cole/Duomo Photography. 23: AFP/Corbis
Corporation

Cover and book design by Lucie Maragni and Agatha Jaspon

ISBN 0-7652-1371-0

Printed in the United States of America

8 9 10   07 06

1-800-321-3106
www.pearsonlearning.com

Contents

For Harry, a great soccer dad

Chapter 1

Soccer Is for Everyone

Do you like to play outside? Do you like to run? Do you like to play with a ball? You can do all of these things if you play soccer.

Boys and girls play soccer. ➡

Soccer players cannot throw and catch the ball. They cannot touch the ball with their hands. Soccer players can only kick the ball.

6

Soccer is played with two teams. There is a goal for each team. Some goals are big nets held up by posts. Other goals are shown by lines that mark a space.

Players on one team want to kick the ball into one goal. Players on the other team want to kick the ball into the other goal. Players score when the ball goes into the other's team's goal. They make one point.

A goalie tries to stop a ball.

Lots of people play soccer. You can be young or old, big or small. Soccer is easy to play. All you need is a ball and a place to play. Then find enough players to make two teams.

Pelé after scoring a goal ▶

Soccer POINT One of the greatest soccer players of all time is Pelé. As a child in Brazil, he practiced soccer with a ball made of rags.

Chapter 2

Playing Soccer

People play soccer on a big grassy field. The field is 100 to 130 yards long and 50 to 100 yards wide. For young players the field is about half that size. The goals are 8 feet high and 24 feet wide.

Layout of a soccer field ➡

Halfway line—

Penalty-kick mark

Penalty area

Center mark

Center circle

Goal area

Goal line

Goal

Corner area

Touchline

Players usually wear shorts and a shirt. Players also wear long socks over shin guards. Shin guards are pads that cover the legs below the knees. They guard the legs against moving balls and kicks.

Players wear special shoes, too. The shoes have points on the bottom. These points help players run on the grass without slipping.

Soccer cleats ⬆

Shin guard ▶

Two teams playing a soccer game ▲

There are 11 players on a soccer team. Teams of young players may have 6 players. During a game, players on a team try to move the ball down the field. Players on the other team try to take the ball away.

Players move the ball by kicking it. Short kicks are called dribbling. A long kick is called a pass.

A goalie blocks a soccer ball. ➤

One player on each team is the goalie. The goalie tries to stop a ball from going into a goal. Only goalies can use their hands to catch the ball.

Soccer POINT

Older, skilled players can hit the ball with their foreheads. This is called heading.

Chapter 3

A Very Old Game

People have played games like soccer for many years. Long ago in Asia, people played with a ball stuffed with hair and bark. They tried to kick the ball between two posts.

◀ A game like soccer has been played in Japan for a long time.

American Indians played a kicking game. ⬆

American Indians also played a kicking game a long time ago. Their ball was made of deerskin. A team could have up to 1,000 players.

Many people believe that soccer started in England over 800 years ago. Crowds kicked a ball through the city streets. Games lasted for hours. Today an adult soccer game takes 90 minutes.

Schoolboys played a game like soccer in England in the 1800s. That was about 200 years ago. Each school made up its own rules. The players called the game football.

Football players could touch the ball with their hands. They could also use their feet. Some players wanted to use only their feet. So players met in 1863 to write rules for soccer.

English soccer game in the 1800s ➡

15

Soccer spread from England to other countries. A group formed in 1904. They made sure that teams around the world followed the same rules. Soccer teams still use these rules.

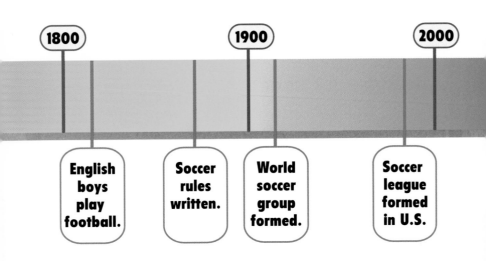

1800 — English boys play football.

Soccer rules written.

1900 — World soccer group formed.

2000 — Soccer league formed in U.S.

Soccer POINT Soccer players must follow the rules and play safely. The referee makes sure they do.

Chapter 4

The Best Soccer

Children and adults play soccer in leagues. Leagues are groups of teams that play against each other. The teams play to find out which team is the best. In a league the players are all about the same age.

Young players march in a soccer parade. ➡

Boys and girls as young as five can play in soccer leagues. The best kids' teams in the country get to play in the US Open Cup. They play against teams from all over the world.

Girls play in the US Open Cup. ➡

Zach Thornton, goalie for an MLS team ▲

Young players can play for high school and college teams. The best players then can join Major League Soccer (MLS) teams. An MLS soccer team is for professional adult players. There are 12 MLS teams in the United States.

The World Cup is the most important event in soccer. Teams from different countries play against each other. There is a World Cup for men. There is another World Cup for women. Both World Cup events are held every four years.

1996 Men's World Cup ➡

Ronaldo
of Brazil

Brazil has won the men's World Cup four times. That's more than any other country. Ronaldo of Brazil is one of the best soccer players. He scored four goals in the 1998 World Cup. He has been voted the World Player of the Year two times.

Mia Hamm ▶

Mia Hamm is one of the best women soccer players in the world. She has scored a world record of over 110 goals. She is on the U.S. Women's National Team. She played in the 1999 Women's World Cup. The United States won.

Players like Ronaldo and Mia Hamm know that soccer is a team sport. No one player wins a game alone. Everyone works together to score. That's why soccer is so much fun to watch and to play.

⬆ **The 1999 U.S. Women's World Cup team holds the winning trophy.**

Soccer POINT

The World Cup trophy was taken in 1966. No one could find it. A dog named Pickles found it in a trash can.

Glossary

dribbling   [DRIHB lihng] moving the ball with short kicks

goal   [gohl] the place where a ball must go to make a point

goalie   [GOH lee] a player who tries to stop the other team's ball from going into the goal

league   [leeg] a group of teams that play against each other

professional   [pruh FESH uh nul] being paid to play a sport or do a job

referee   [REF uh ree] a person who makes sure a game is being played fairly and safely

score   [skor] to make a point in a game

trophy   [TROH fee] anything given as a prize for winning